W9-BKS-822

PAYDAY!

KATHRYN BEATON

Published in the United States of America by Cherry Lake Publishing
Ann Arbor, Michigan
www.cherrylakepublishing.com

Math Education: Dr. Timothy Whiteford, Associate Professor of Education at St. Michael's College
Financial Adviser: Kenneth Klooster, financial adviser at Edward Jones Investments
Reading Adviser: Marla Conn, ReadAbility Inc.

Photo Credits: © Will Rodrigues/Shutterstock Images, cover, 1, 7; © Andrey_Popov/Shutterstock Images, cover, 1; © Fuse/Thinkstock Images, 5; © Artwell/Shutterstock Images, 9; © Blue_Cutler/iStock.com, 11; © S_L/Shutterstock Images, 13; © Chad Mcdermott/Thinkstock Images, 15; © LSOphoto/iStock.com, 17; © Samuel Borges Photography/Shutterstock Images, 19; © Melinda Millward, 21; © Suzanne Tucker/Shutterstock Images, 22; © Monkey Business Images/Shutterstock Images, 25; © Catalin Petolea/Shutterstock Images, 27; © lzf/Shutterstock Images, 28

Library of Congress Cataloging-in-Publication Data

Beaton, Kathryn.
    Payday! / Kathryn Beaton.
    pages cm. — (Real world math: personal finance)
    Includes index.
    ISBN 978-1-63362-573-0 (hardcover) — ISBN 978-1-63362-753-6 (pdf) — ISBN 978-1-63362-663-8 (pbk.) — ISBN 978-1-63362-843-4 (ebook) 1. Finance, Personal—Juvenile literature. 2. Income—Juvenile literature. 3. Money—Juvenile literature. I. Title.

HG179.B352 2016
332.024—dc23   2015001404

Cherry Lake Publishing would like to acknowledge the work of the Partnership for 21st Century Skills. Please visit www.p21.org for more information.

Printed in the United States of America
Corporate Graphics

ABOUT THE AUTHOR

Kathryn Beaton lives and writes in Ann Arbor, Michigan.

TABLE OF CONTENTS

CHAPTER 1

BIG DREAMS

Take a moment now and imagine your future. Do you see yourself wearing designer clothes and driving a fancy car? Will you be living in a mansion on the beach? Maybe you will have a sailboat or a few horses. Right now, it's fun to dream about these things. But when you grow up, you'll have to pay for your house, car, and clothes. That means getting a job.

Do you get an **allowance**? Allowances often increase as children grow up and can do more difficult chores to earn the money. James, age 5, gets $2.00 a week. He can do simple tasks. He might set the table or help put away groceries. Vanessa, age 9, receives $6.00 a week. She can do harder tasks. She might vacuum, wash the car, or take out the recycling. The allowances James and Vanessa receive are related to how much they can help.

Many parents give their kids allowances, but the amount depends on how old they are.

Adults are also paid according to what they do. Many jobs pay by the hour, like working as a cashier or sales associate. A job requiring few skills pays a low hourly rate. A job requiring more skills pays a higher rate. A worker who stays with the same company for a long time might get a **raise**.

The U.S. Congress sets the **minimum** amount that businesses have to pay their **employees** for every hour worked. Since 2009, the national minimum wage has been $7.25 per hour. It's illegal for an **employer** to pay an employee less than that amount. State governments can also set their own minimum wage. As of 2015, the state of Washington has the highest, at $9.47 per hour.

People in some jobs are paid a **salary**. Their paychecks are the same amount every time, even if the hours vary. Salaried jobs, like being an engineer or an editor, generally require more education. These jobs usually come with **benefits**. Benefits are extra things, such as health insurance and life insurance, that the

Receiving your first paycheck can be exciting!

employer pays for. A job with benefits gives the employee a certain number of vacation days, too. Some employers also put money into their employees' retirement accounts, where it will accumulate **interest**.

One big difference between high- and low-paying jobs is the level of education you need to do the job. To become a lawyer, doctor, or teacher, you'll need many years of college classes. Other times, people learn a specific skill at a **vocational** school. For example, they might study

21ST CENTURY CONTENT

Are you planning on being a superstar on an NFL team? The competition is stiff. As of 2014, more than 1.1 million high school boys play football in the United States. But even if you're one of the 25,000 to 30,000 college football players on school rosters each season, the NFL only hires about 250 new players in its annual draft. You do the math—better keep practicing!

Working at a coffee shop is a popular job for young people.

plumbing or restaurant management. Other people, such as truck drivers, advance in their careers through on-the-job training, where they gain experience. Some jobs don't require a high school diploma. These jobs, such as being a janitor or a store clerk, often pay very little and usually don't include benefits.

Can't wait to get that first big paycheck? There are a few things you need to know about how much money you'll actually take home.

CHAPTER 2

You Have A Paycheck— Now What?

You landed that dream job. Now it's payday! Most employers pay their workers every two weeks.

For salaried jobs, you can take your annual salary and divide it by 12 to get your **gross monthly pay**. But don't expect the entire gross monthly pay to end up in your bank account. When you get an allowance, the whole amount is yours, even if your parents restrict how you can use it. But unlike an allowance, a paycheck comes with **deductions**. Deductions are amounts subtracted from paychecks before the worker

Treating a broken bone can be expensive if you aren't covered by insurance.

gets the money. Federal, state, and local taxes are deductions.

Deductions also include payments for health insurance. Health insurance pays for medical expenses and sometimes for dental and vision care. This means that when you go for an appointment, you only pay a small fee, called a co-pay, instead of the full cost of the visit. Without health insurance, taking care of a brief illness or minor injury could be very expensive.

Everyone pays **Social Security tax** and **Medicare tax**. This money is put in reserve for you to use when you retire or if you become disabled. Some people also have deductions for money that is put into a retirement account. Some companies allow you to have donations to charities, such as United Way, taken directly from your paycheck.

REAL WORLD MATH CHALLENGE

Alan just got his first monthly paycheck. His gross monthly pay is $2,000.00. Listed below are his deductions.

Deductions

Federal income tax $140.19
Social Security and Medicare tax $136.02
State income tax $78.27
City income tax $9.96
Health insurance $33.06
Retirement account $75.00
Humane Society $25.00

- How much money does Alan have left to deposit in his bank account?

(Turn to page 30 for the answers)

GROSS
TOTAL TAXES W/H 63
32.64
TOTAL OTHER TAXES
.00
TOTAL VOL. DED.
60.48
NET PAY
224.51

Your paycheck will show the amount of taxes taken out.

Spending most of your paycheck right after you get it might leave you with very little money to spend until the next one. What happens if your friend invites you to a baseball game, but you won't get paid for five more days? You remember that you used some of your last paycheck to pay your dad part of your phone bill, and some to buy flowers for your mom's birthday. Those were important expenses, but what happened to the rest of the money? You don't have enough left to buy a ticket to the game. How do you make sure this doesn't happen again? Let's find out!

21ST CENTURY CONTENT

Federal, state, and local taxes pay for things everyone shares, such as highways, public schools, and parks. Everyone must pay federal income tax, but state income taxes vary. Different states have different tax rates. Nine states don't tax your earnings at all. Also, some cities charge income tax, which are called local taxes.

If you're careful about where your money goes, you'll be able to spend it on special events every now and then.

CHAPTER 3

Do the Math: Keep Track of Spending

Creating a **budget** can help you make the right choices. A budget is a plan for how you'll spend your money. To create a budget, you need to know your income and your expenses.

What's your income? Do you get an allowance in exchange for chores you do around the house? This is income you receive on a regular basis. What are your expenses? Expenses are the things you spend money on. People like to spend money on different things. You might spend your money as soon as you get it, but maybe your sister holds on to hers until there's something she really needs. Before you can make a budget, you need to figure out your spending patterns.

Babysitting is a popular way for teenagers to make money.

One way to keep track is to get a small notepad. (You can also use the note-taking feature on your phone.) Every time you buy something, no matter how small, write down the item and the amount. Do this for two weeks. It will give you some good ideas about how you're spending your money. After two weeks, look to see where your money went. Surprised? Maybe there's a way to spend more carefully.

Make a list of categories: Food, Entertainment, Clothes, Transportation, Charity, and Other. Put every item that you spend money on in one of these categories. Now what do you do with this list?

21ST CENTURY CONTENT

According to a 2014 survey by the Harris Poll, most kids in the United States get between $5.00 and $10.00 per week for allowance. The amount depends on a variety of factors, including the kids' ages, their parents' ages, and where they live.

*A guitar is expensive enough that you would
need to budget your money before buying it.*

REAL WORLD MATH CHALLENGE

Joanna is saving to start learning guitar. The guitar she wants costs $50.00.
She receives $6.00 a week for her allowance. Last week, she bought a note-
book ($1.95), a candy bar ($0.60), and some nail polish ($0.95). She put the
rest in the bank to save for the guitar.

- If Joanna puts the same amount in the bank each week, how long will it
take for her to get her guitar?
- How long will it take if she also saves the $25.00 her grandma gives her
for her birthday?

(Turn to page 30 for the answers)

Do the Math: Create a Budget

You've made a list of everything you bought in the last two weeks. Now you need to look at how you spent your money. Did you make a lot of little purchases? Or maybe you only bought two or three things, but they were expensive. Look at each item on that list. Did you need to buy it, or did you just want it?

To save up for more expensive items, you need to cut down on what you spend now. Think about items on the list that you wanted but didn't need. Maybe you bought a great baseball cap, but you already have seven of them.

Monthly Budget Worksheet			
CATEGORY	BUDGET AMOUNT	ACTUAL AMOUNT	DIFFERENCE
Income:			
Allowance - for month	$40		
Baby sitting	$20		
extra chores	$20		
Expenses:			
movie night		$30	
baseball game			
jeans			

A simple chart can help you see the patterns in your spending habits.

Are you glad you spent this money? Would you be just as happy if you hadn't? To make a budget, you have to decide what's important to you.

When creating a budget, think about big purchases you want to make. That pair of jeans you want costs $30.00, but your allowance is only $10.00 a week. You're going to have to put aside some money every week if you want to buy the jeans. This is a short-term goal. And what about your class trip to Boston in the spring? Your parents say you need to pay for half the expenses. That's a long-term goal.

Raking leaves for your neighbors can be a good way to earn extra money.

Sometimes, you need extra money quickly but your allowance for the week is gone. If you ask your parents for next week's allowance early, you won't have it later. The best way to handle emergencies is to plan ahead. When you're making your budget, set aside some money as an emergency fund. Add to it each week. That way, when something unexpected comes up, such as if you ruin your brother's favorite shoes and have to replace them, you have enough money to cover it.

So now you've decided which things matter to you and how much you can afford to spend on them. You've thought about your long- and short-term goals. You want to put money away for emergencies and give money to charity.

Now you're ready to write down your budget. Say your weekly allowance is $15.00. Write that at the top of the

LIFE AND CAREER SKILLS

How do you know which things are wants and which things are needs? It can be hard to tell the difference. If you're thirsty at a restaurant, you can usually get water for free. That will satisfy the need. If you buy a supersize soda instead, that's because you want the soda. Both water and soda will help you enjoy your meal more, but one is free and the other costs money. A good compromise is to buy a small soda that will quench your thirst at half the cost (and maybe you can still get free refills!). To make good decisions about your budget, you have to be honest about whether you really need something or only want it.

REAL WORLD MATH CHALLENGE

Aditi's allowance is $7.00 a week. She also receives $5.00 a week for babysitting. Every month, she gives money to an animal shelter. She is saving money for a trip her family is taking next summer to Hawaii. She also wants to go to a concert next month and go shopping with her sister, Jen. So many places to spend her money! It's time to set up a budget. She decides to donate 10 percent of her income to charity. She will save 15 percent for long-term goals and 25 percent for short-term goals. The remaining 50 percent of her income is spending money.

- What's Aditi's weekly income?
- How much does she set aside for charity?
- How much for short- and long-term goals?
- How much does Aditi have to spend on shopping with Jen?

(Turn to page 30 for the answers)

page. Then write down how much you're going to spend on expenses—maybe $9.00, split between food and entertainment. You're also putting away $3.00 for a new skateboard. The emergency fund will get $1.50, and $1.50 goes into the charity fund. You've done it! You've created a budget.

Sometimes, though, it's tough to stick to a budget. You'd like to have a little more money to work with. What can you do? Let's find out!

Your parents might set a budget for grocery shopping.

LIFE AND CAREER SKILLS

Making a budget is personal. Your parents and friends can give you advice, but they might prioritize things differently than you do. Listen to them, but in the end, you will have to decide what works for your income and lifestyle.

CHAPTER 5

GETTING AHEAD

Sometimes your allowance isn't enough to buy what you want. You don't want to wipe out all of your savings either. What can you do?

If you feel you deserve it, try **negotiating** with your parents for more money. Keep in mind that when you negotiate, both sides usually have to give a little. Your parents might agree to give you a higher allowance, but it might not be as much as you want. And remember, if you accept more money, you'll probably have to do more chores. Think first about the chores you normally do for

If you want a bigger allowance, try talking to your parents about why you deserve it.

your allowance. If you usually take out the trash, maybe you could also sort the recycling. Once you've made a list of some extra jobs, figure out what you think is a fair payment for each one.

Choose a time to talk when your parents are not busy doing something else. Sit down with them and explain your side. Give them the list of jobs and prices. Ask them if there's something on the list that they would like to hire you to do. Then negotiate a price that you all think is fair. If you have a specific goal you're saving money for,

Many stores offer coupons that they send out through texts.

you can explain to your parents why it's important to you. If they see that you're responsible enough to plan ahead, they might be more willing to give you opportunities to earn the money you need.

If these chores go well at your house, try asking your neighbors if they need help, too! You can distribute flyers with your name, services, and prices.

Another way to make your allowance last longer is to look around for the best price on a specific item. If you or your parents have a smartphone, a lot of apps can help you find something for the cheapest price. Maybe the video game you want at the store where you are is $30.00, but if you walk to the store across the street, you can buy it there for $25.00. Look online, too—you may be able to buy it on Amazon or eBay for an even lower price. Being patient can help you save money!

You work hard for your money. By planning ahead, using a budget, and shopping carefully, you'll get the most out of your hard-earned paycheck.

Real World Math Challenge

Lucy is saving up for a new mountain bike. She has saved $226.89. She needs another $72.00. Her parents agree to pay her to do extra chores on the weekend. They will give her $4.00 an hour for doing the laundry and washing the car, or $6.00 an hour for raking leaves while also keeping an eye on her little sister. She will work two hours every Saturday.

- How long will it take her to earn the remaining money for the bike if she does the laundry and washes the car, if she works two hours every Saturday?
- How long will it take if she babysits and rakes the leaves?

(Turn to page 30 for the answers)

REAL WORLD MATH CHALLENGE ANSWERS

CHAPTER TWO
Page 12
The total of the deductions is $497.50.
$140.19 + $136.02 + $78.27 + $9.96 + $33.06 +
$75.00 + $25.00 = $497.50
Alan's paycheck, after the deductions,
will be $1,502.50.
$2,000 − $497.50 = $1,502.50

CHAPTER THREE
Page 19
Joanna spent $3.50.
$1.95 + $0.60 + $0.95 = $3.50
Joanna saves $2.50 each week.
$6.00 − $3.50 = $2.50
If she uses only money from her allowance, it will take
Joanna 20 weeks to save enough money for her guitar.
$50.00 ÷ $2.50 = 20

If she saves her grandma's gift, Joanna still will need
$25.00. It will take her 10 weeks to save that much
from her allowance.
$50.00 − $25.00 = $25.00
$25.00 ÷ $2.50 = 10

CHAPTER FOUR
Page 24
Aditi's income is $12.00 per week.
$7.00 + $5.00 = $12.00

Aditi will give $1.20 to charity, save $1.80 for
long-term goals, and save $3.00 for short-term goals.
She has $6.00 to spend shopping with Jen.
10% of $12.00 = .10 x $12.00 = $1.20
15% of $12.00 = .15 x $12.00 = $1.80
25% of $12.00 = .25 x $12.00 = $3.00
50% of $12.00 = .50 x $12.00 = $6.00

CHAPTER FIVE
Page 29
Lucy would earn $8.00 a week doing the laundry and
washing the car. She would earn $12.00 a week
babysitting her sister and raking leaves.
2 x $4.00 = $8.00
2 x $6.00 = $12.00
It would take Lucy 9 weeks to earn the money for the
bike doing laundry and washing the car. If she
babysits her sister and rakes leaves, it will take her
only 6 weeks.
$72.00 ÷ $8.00 = 9
$72.00 ÷ $12.00 = 6

FIND OUT MORE

BOOKS

Harman, Hollis Page. *Money Sense for Kids*. Hauppauage, NY: Barron's Educational Series, 2005.

Vermond, Kira, and Clayton Hanmer. *The Secret Life of Money: A Kid's Guide to Cash*. Toronto: Owlkids Books, 2012.

WEB SITES

Social Studies for Kids—Want vs. Need: Basic Economics
www.socialstudiesforkids.com/articles/economics/wantsandneeds1.htm
Read this page to learn how to tell the difference between something you want and something you need.

YouTube: Biz Kid$ 1.25 Understanding Your Paycheck
http://youtu.be/o4iYWixBLIM
Watch this episode of the PBS show Biz Kid$ to learn about paychecks.

GLOSSARY

allowance (uh-LOU-uhns) money given to someone regularly, especially from parents to a child

benefits (BEN-uh-fits) extra things that an employer pays for other than wages

budget (BUHJ-it) a plan for how money will be earned, spent, and saved

deductions (dih-DUK-shunz) money subtracted from a paycheck for taxes and benefits

employees (em-ploi-EEZ) people who do jobs for someone else

employer (em-PLOI-ur) one who hires others to do a job

gross monthly pay (GROHS MUHNTH-lee PAY) income before deductions

interest (IN-trist) the amount earned on money kept in a bank

Medicare tax (MEH-dih-kayr TAKS) a tax used to pay for a government-funded health insurance program, especially for those over age 65

minimum (MIN-uh-muhm) the least amount possible

negotiating (nih-GO-shee-ate-eng) discussing with others ways to reach an agreement

raise (RAYZ) an increase in salary

salary (SAH-luh-ree) a fixed amount of money a worker is paid for services

Social Security tax (SO-shul sih-KYUR-uh-tee TAKS) a tax used to pay for a government-funded retirement program

vocational (voh-KAY-shuh-nul) related to training in a specific trade

INDEX